Arts Holding H
(AHHAH)

Arts Holding Hands and Hearts, a 501.3c non-profit organization, has served Chester County, PA. youths in Coatesville and Kennett Square since 2013. Its mission is to empower youth, strengthen families, and mobilize communities through arts, literacy, and mindfulness. Its programs simultaneously promote social and racial equity and justice.

arts holding hands and hearts, inc

www.AHHAH.org

JUSTICE RESTORED 3.0

Edited by Zandra Matthews

Bushwick Writer Publishing

Bushwick Writer Publishing
www.bushwickwriter.com
Cover by Jaleah, L.N., J., and D.
All rights reserved
ISBN: 9798833948026

TABLE OF CONTENTS

Dedication

We dedicate this book to juveniles in the justice system whose voices have been marginalized and to all juveniles who feel lost, misguided, or misunderstood.

Dario Duran

The less you know the better.
Just know I'm better than ever.
Jazlyn

FORWARD

In 2013 Arts Holding Hands and Hearts (AHHAH) began working with incarcerated youth at the Chester County Youth Center (CCYC). The facility houses homeless and abused girls ages 10 to 18 as well as a detention center for boys and girls of the same age. AHHAH's workshops employ trauma sensitive yoga techniques that immediately and positively effect juveniles. The program also establishes camaraderie. The participants are encouraged to write about their lives—their family, friends, schools, and community. Since 2013, the AHHAH workshops have produced over 1,000 poems, short stories, memoirs, and letters. *Justice Restored 3.0.* showcases a selection of them which were subsequently illustrated by Chester County Futures high school students from Oxford, Kennett Square, and Coatesville. The result? *Justice Restored 3.0*, an illustrated collection of poignant personal stories from inside and outside Chester County's juvenile youth system.

As the founder of AHHAH, I hope the reader of this small book will take in its powerful words and be moved by the artistic responses of the peer illustrators. I hope instead of asking, "What did these kids do?", the reader asks, "What took place in their homes, schools or communities that led to their distress and incarceration?" I hope the fifty paired texts and images spark compassion and, I hope, prompt you the reader/the viewer to actively promote a more equitable society and social system for our youths. Young people need to believe they can thrive.

My mantra for them…and for you…

May you know that you are not alone in your pain and suffering.
May you be Safe and Protected
May you be Healthy and Strong
May you be Happy and Content
May you live with Peace and at Ease
May you be Free.

Jan Michener
Founder, Executive Director, Arts Holding Hands and Hearts (AHHAH)

WHO AM I

Black Beautiful Girl

By Ni'Ajah, a 14-year-old girl in the shelter at CCYC

I am a Black, Beautiful, Girl.
Who was once scared of the world,
I used to be scared to face the world of hate.
I opened a gate,
So I can face world of great.
You can't hurt me,
Not even unlock me.
I come from a place,
That felt like a locked cage,
And no, it ain't never got replaced,
And no, it never changed me one bit,
And no, you not gonna call me a liar.
When you look at me you see
Black, Beautiful, Girl.
And the way I act is not great,
But, Yes I opened up a gate
So all the hate that never got the take.
If only you could see the true me,
The talented bright me.
I'm not gonna hide behind a tree forever,
Cause I've been put together.
One day people will say,
"She was a beautiful girl, who was scared to face the world of HATE,
But Explored it and now she feels so GREAT."
I AM A BLACK, BEAUTIFUL, GIRL

Beautiful Black Girl

Drawing by Saniya Holmes-Cooper

Title: Beautiful Black Queen

Beautiful Black Girl

Drawing by Sanaia Harris

Beautiful Black Girl

Drawing by Chester County Futures Student

I AM Jordan

By Jordan, a youth in CCYC 10/23/20

I am from Coatesville
But moved recently.
My first house left an imprint on me.
The sounds in my neighborhood,
Quiet and sometimes loud.
I hang out with my friend Michael.
High point – winning football game
Low point – being in CCYC.
My goal is to play football,
Get an education,
And become a vet.
From my pain I have learned not to give up
Even though I may want to give up
Because if I give up,
Then it would just be me messing up
all my chances for success.
For me to get where I want to go
I need a fresh start.
One day,
People will cheer!
One day,
I will say,
I've come a long way
And I'm Here!

Reflections on workshop: I feel hopeful, In my body I feel tired, I am surprised by how far I've come, I wonder what will happen in my life/future.

I Am Jordan

Drawing by Jaleah

I Am

By Nakai

I am a good kid.
I am smart.
I am respectful.
I am a strong person of faith.
The best about the future is that it comes only one day at a time.
Remember who you are.
Don't compromise for anyone

I Am

Drawing by Claudia Vara

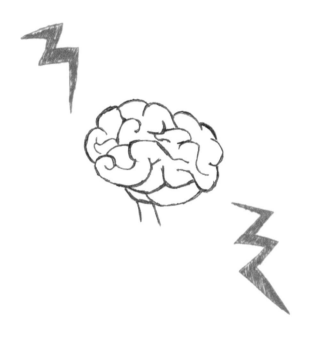

A Girl Who Struggles

By Cesaly, a 16-year-old girl in the shelter at CCYC

When you look at me you see a 16-year-old girl who struggles.

A girl who's made bad decisions.

A girl with a bad reputation.

A girl who's misunderstood.

Most importantly, a girl who dealt with everything and anything.

I have a secret, I'm not perfect.

I've made some very bad mistakes.

I've been through a lot.

I've been to many places,

And still haven't gotten better, physically.

I remember a time I would help my mother cook and clean.

I would tell her everything and anything.

We would laugh about what happened the day before or just something random.

Another thing I remember is getting yelled at.

My 8-year-old self really didn't know what to say or do.

I was frightened and worried what would happen next.

A time I said yes is when my mom taught me manners.

She taught me to respond with "yes".

I have a dream to go to college or beauty school,

Then start a family and become a family.

I want to live a better life.

I want to have children

And let my children know what their mother has been through

And I would make sure they won't go through it.

About this workshop: My aha moment today is how open I was

A Girl Who Struggles

Drawing by Michaella Remy

Do You See Me?

By Taylor M., a 17-year-old girl in the shelter at CCYC

When you look at me you see fear

For what the future holds,
Anxiety caused by anything I cannot for see.
What if I told you,
You are just like me.
One day I will be what I aim to be,
Have a future and finally be happy.
Do you see me when I'm locked up,
Out of sight, out of harms' way,
No longer lurking with the night?
Does my family realize me when I am around,
Able to finally comprehend sight and sound?
Do people recognize me on the streets when
I'm with my friends walking around,
Playing pretend?
If people could only see me when I'm finally at Zen,
No act,
Just me and my pen.
If people could see behind these eyes they would see
A Bitter World,
Yet with so much beauty,
But locked up with a hidden key.
Will they see me if I can no longer be seen,
Apart from pictures or videos and distant memories?
DO YOU SEE ME?

Do You See Me?

Drawing by Rubyt Luna-Hernandez

Title: See Me

Sometimes I Feel Like

By Jasmine, a girl in the shelter at CCYC

Sometimes I feel like a pit bull
Because I am protective over my family,
Because I attack,
Because I want to be loved.
Sometimes I feel like a volcano
Because I'm steady,
Because I can't stop going when I'm angry,
Because I get heated.
Sometimes I feel like a tiger
Because I attack,
Because I zoom out quickly,
Because I'm fearless.
Sometimes I feel like a panda
Because I'm sweet,
Because I'm warm hearted,
Because I want to be hugged.

Sometimes I Feel Like

Drawing by Alazia Hudnell

Sometimes I Feel Like

Drawing by April Aguliera

Sometimes I Feel Like

Drawing by Osmary Martinez Rosa

Title: Jungle Of Thoughts

WHERE I COME FROM

Nakai's Own Words

A 13-year-old in Detention

Chapter One.

I never thought I would make it considering my past, but before we get into that, I want to tell the world how I made it. I had a rough upbringing. My father left my mother before I was born. I have never seen or spoken to him. My mother raised my brother and I by herself. She tried, but we never had a stable living environment. We bounced from home to home, but she made sacrifices for us to maintain. Often times, she would go without eating, but made sure that my brother and I had food in our belly. Without having much of an education, and two kids before she was 16 years old, I guess she did the best that she could. Because we moved around so much, I seldom went to school. It became normal to miss weeks at a time. When my brother, who was three years older than me, reached middle school, his grandfather was granted custody of him. I was left alone with no other family to count on. Shortly after, child protective services removed me from my home and I was placed in foster care. I bounced from foster home to foster home. Then, I went to Fairmont Mental Health Hospital. Then, I went to another foster home. Then, I went to Belmont Hospital. Then, Deveroeux. I was there for two-and-a-half years. I made friends. I fought a lot and I got serious charges. Now, I am at CCYC trying to survive. I am learning from my mistakes. I am 13 and I have a lot to learn. I wrote letters to my aunts saying, "I will do better, I know better, and I will be a role model." I love setting examples for younger children and sometimes reading Ruby Bridges books. She inspires me to be a role model. I am committed to succeeding in life. I want to support my family. I value family a lot. To everybody I inspire, I want them to do their best and learn from their mistakes.

Chapter Two.

I can't be with my mom because she lost her rights over me until I'm 18. It's hard to bear knowing we will be apart from each other for that long, but in the situation I'm in now, I can't show emotion. I can't seem or act weak. I've learned a lot since being here. A quote I've heard has stuck to me and it inspires me on a daily basis. It's from Abl. He said, "The best thing about the future is that it comes only one day at a time." I miss my mother a lot and even though I can't speak to her, I manage to sneak a quick conversation with her. My grandma just informed me I have a little brother, now. She's always worrying about me and writes me on a daily basis. Being here makes me feel weak. I was once a man of the house and was stiffed from that. I can't protect my family like I wish I could. It hurts me.

Crying in Pain

By Dylan, a 17-year-old in Detention

How can I become a man,
When I'm from the Poor.
My life growing up
Was devastating and hard.
Being beat and abused
Growing through tragedy.
Brother going through a glass storm door
At age 5.
I was 11
When I saw my brother almost die,
Covered in blood.
My heart almost stopped
Seeing my whole family
Crying in Pain.

Reflections on workshop: I feel that I can express my feelings and not be judged for it. This group makes me very happy and I can be myself.

Crying In Pain

Drawing by Kiara Carillo

Title: Slipping Through the Cracks

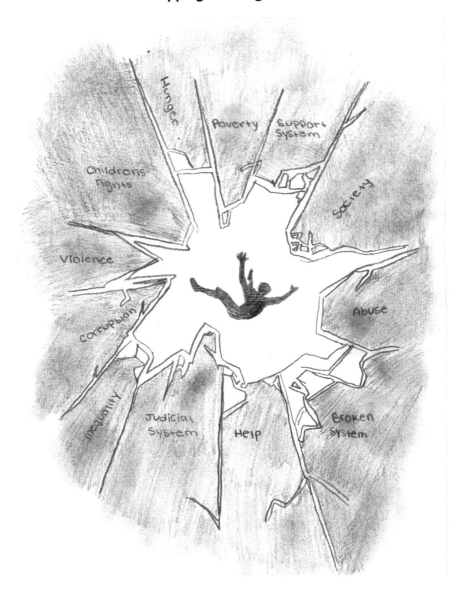

Crying In Pain

Drawings by Alexandria Monroy

- hurt, shame, pain

- Trauma

Crying In Pain

Drawing by Jaleah

Chapter One

By Donnie, age 19, a youth in detention at CCYC

Do you know what I overcame?
I overcame the bullies,
The abuse,
The loss of family and close friends.
You're going to know my name
Cause I'm going to get off probation,
Go to the navy,
Follow my Dad's family's footstep.
Get married,
Have a happy family
Without worrying about the
Pain and Depression
I've gone through,
All the struggles I've been through.
Try not to go into the negatives.
I overcame
Everything in my life.
Trying to avoid the shame,
Light the flame inside me.
I rewrote the game.
Chapter One:
My Life
How I came
This far.

Chapter One

Drawing by Chester County Futures Student

Where I Come From and Where I'm Going

By Seamus, a 16-year-old in detention at CCYC

My room is my room.
It is located in West Chester, PA.
My walls are covered with a tapestry of a tree,
A Chance, the rapper poster also on the wall.
My bed is on the floor and is never made
And the TV is broken as well as the door, from my fist.
Cooper Smith Park and the woods at that park
Is where I spent a lot of time growing up.
I went to camp as a young kid and made forts in the woods as I grew
older.
In the park a lot of old people walking,
A lot of people walking babies.
There are lots of dogs barking
and some cars stroll by occasionally.

Christmas stands out the most for me.
We usually have a nice big ham, cooked to perfection by my Pop Pop.
On the kitchen counter is a delicious pumpkin pie.

I've really been on my own for the past 3 years.
I always looked up to my dad, he taught me a lot.
When I was 14, he passed away.
I had no choice, so I started doing things on my own.
I grew up hearing,
You're wise beyond your years.
Don't do drugs.
Stay in school.

My Pops passing away from cancer messed me up.
I will push myself to make him proud.
I know he is watching me from Heaven.
I will not settle until I get off probation.

My mom gives me energy to keep going in life and keep pushing.
I have courage to keep going.
I want to get a good education.
I want to have a happy family.
One day people will say about me,
"He was a really good father to his children."
No matter what happens,
Life goes on
And everything happens for a reason.

Reflection of workshop: I realized that I need to get out of places like this so I can show people I'm going to do good.

Where I'm From

By Serenity, a 15-year-old girl in detention

What is coming is better
Than what's going.
I'm from a city where they show no love.
In a city full of rats,
Heard people plotting on me,
Gotta watch my back.
People in the struggle
Stuck hustling
Just to stay up.
You don't know me.
You don't know my life.
You don't know what's happened.
Life is tragic.
My life,
Dad's in jail.
Mom at home stressing.
When you look at me
You see
Innocent girl,
Pain in my eyes,
Pretty smile.
I am.....

Reflections on Workshop: "Something little can go a long way."

I'm From

By Shaheed, a 15-year-old in detention at CCYC

I'm from York
Loud music
Kids playing
Adults laughing and joking.
I'm from
Bake Mac, fried chicken, yams, mashed potatoes, corn.
I'm from
Mom, dad, sister, friends, brothers and cousins.
I'm from
"I'ma give you sum to cry about"
"You gon be dead or in jail"
I wonder when I will go home.
When I failed 2nd grade
I learned to keep pushing forward.
I won't settle til I go home.
Family gives me strength.
Friends give me courage.
I want happiness and to be a professional athlete.
My family will help me.
One day people will say,
"He was an innocent man"
And I will say
"Thank You"
I am determined.

I Am From

By Shaun a 14-year-old in detention at CCYC

I am from
Knives, music, albums,
Neat room, made bed, desk,
Shell casings, deer head.
I come from a home that makes me happy
And comfortable to be myself.
I come from
Police sirens, drugs, women, teenagers playing football, adults playing
basketball.
My amazing roommate, my fiancé, my guidance counselor
My dad, my mom, my grandfather, my aunt
Have shaped who I am today.
I grew up hearing
Actions speak louder than words.
If you don't have something nice to say, don't say it at all.
Someone told me I would never be someone and I would never get a
job.
I grew up and got a job and made more money than them.
I will not settle until I have made a difference in this world.
My fiancé gives me strength.
My dad gives me courage.
I want to make this place a safe environment
I want to be a construction worker.
One day people will say that I made a difference.
One day I will say, "I have bettered myself."

*Reflections of workshop: I am feeling motivated right now. I am
surprised by all the things that I have overcome and what I am
working on overcoming.*

YOUTH VOICES

Freefall

By Wesley, a youth in detention in CCYC 4/24/18

I wonder where I'll be.
I wonder if I'll stop moving.
If I'll find one place on earth to call Home.
I want to know what the importance to my life will be.
Have I ever helped someone further their life?
Do I really leave a storm behind me everywhere I go?
Will my parents be proud?

I feel out of place.
A tugging train with no track
left to pull my cargo onward with.
A pinball in the machine.
No way to reach my end goal.
A constant push and shove.
Like the tides of the ocean.
Relentless on the shore.
And only a hundred years of this work
will gain me a lonesome inch towards my goal.

I feel stuck.
Like a constant freefall.
Always with the fear of reaching the ground
with all the pent- up force.
But never releasing.

Freefall

Drawing by Nany

Title: Fallen Angel

What Should I Do?

By Wesley, a 17-year-old in detention

I'm surprised that I still care so much
For those that hurt me the most.
I felt so much for her.
I still care so much for her.
But shouldn't I hate her after what happened?
Shouldn't I be angry?
Shouldn't she be at Blame?
Yet, that's not how I feel.
Her eyes still make the oceans stand still.
Her voice still calms me more than any of the places that I've seen.
I still see her face when I close my eyes.
I love her.
I should hate her.
I need her,
Even though she's poison.
I'm stuck.
I want to reach out.
But I know I'll get bit.
It's hard for me to believe that I feel this way.
But I do.
Yet the question is,
What Should I Do?

What Should I Do?

Drawing by Faith Sload

My Life

By Marcus, a 16-year-old in detention at CCYC

I keep repeating the same cycle.
No one listening.
Judge yapping,
"You don't move me."
Keep getting restrained.
Wrote me up
"Going to Keep you for Life"
"Why haven't you changed?"
"What do you care about?"
I don't care.
"What about your freedom?"
You aren't going to play in my mind.
He threatened me.
He wanted me to break down.
Who went before me must have made him mad!
His mind was made up.
Got in trouble 3 times.
First time cool.
Second time home arrest.
Third time now threatening life.
That's how it all happened.
I got restrained.
Lost my loved one.
Being tough, restrained me.
Had that feeling in my gut.
Said I was a smart ass.
Some people are afraid of change.
Started faking it until I make it.
I was really liking doing good

But then I got locked back up.

I only had two more months.

Said he was taking my home pass.

This was on a Wednesday.

I was supposed to leave on a Thursday.

He said he was taking my home pass.

I left.

I got caught with pills.

In my head

Jump out of the car and run.

I could have run to my uncle's house

I was thinking I would get more time if I run.

Home at my uncles

Fight with a white boy

Cops arrived

Got arrested for "aggravated assault with deadly weapon".

What white boy said wasn't matching up

To what happened.

Plea deal.

"If you plead guilty

Will take away deadly weapon.

Misdemeanor instead of felony."

Took deal.

Locked up,

Restrained,

Padded room,

Solitary.

My Life

Drawing by Peyton Weaver

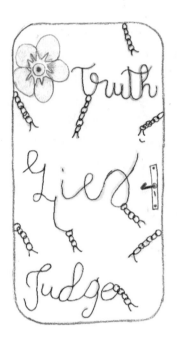

Flower Symbolism
Betrayal, Dishonesty, Disappointment

2.11.2020

By Derek

Been called a demon, called a devil and a fake

I'm not an idol, not an angel, or a saint

I walk alone, I always have

I'm not ashamed

A living nightmare

From the cradle to the grave

Love Poem

By Marcus

Oh, how do I love thee
Let me count the days
I love you like a water ice who finds a peaceful world
I'd take the clouds out of the sky and use them to make a love bed
Every day I like to dream about you
When you said, "Hey,"
My heart started to beat like a drum line

Love Poem

By Richard C.

Oh, how do I love thee
Let me count the girls in my iMessages
I love you like a brother, who finds a dog in the bowl of ice
I'd like to take the clouds out of the sky and use them to make a
glass of mile
Every day, I like to sing about you
When you said, "Birds don't fly,"
My heart started to back flip
Like a professional dancer

Love Poem

Drawing by Jocelyn E and Estrella M.

You Don't Know Me

By Jazlyn, a 16-year-old transgender girl in detention

You don't know me.
You don't want to know me.
The less you know the better.
Just know I'm better than ever.
When you look at me
You see what I used to be
Before the glitz and glam.
They once called me a man,
Before the hair and nails,
The heels along the stairs.
Needles flowed from here to there,
Just to give me longer hair.
Now I'm happy.
But life still isn't fair.

Reflections on workshop: "I'm feeling like I'm touching the f..king ceiling!"

You Don't Know Me

Drawing by Griselle

Reflection on Dr. Martin Luther King Quote

By Omar, a youth in detention at CCYC

Dr. Martin Luther King said,
"What is worse than bad people doing bad things
Is good people standing silently by doing nothing."

There was a South Park episode where the devil said,
"Without bad there wouldn't be good so sometimes it's good to be
bad."

I like Dr. King's quote
Because if someone doesn't speak up or do something about bad being
done
Then they are just letting more people get victimized.

I wonder why people choose to judge a book by its cover.
I want people to know I am capable of things
But that doesn't define me.
People need to know me,
Meet me,
Hangout with me,
Talk to me,
To get to know the real me
And know my morals
And why I act the way I do.

When You Look At Me

A Youth in Detention at CCYC

When you look at me
You see a crime.
See
And me,
Just a caring person.
At last,
Want to do good
For my family.
People see a damned little boy
With a gun charge.
And think that I'm going to end up getting killed
Or life in jail.
But
I just got caught with the wrong people.
When you Look at Me

When you look at me

Brian, a youth in CCYC detention writing for his 6-year-old brother

You see a fun, strong and smart giant.
But when I leave
I change my look.
You want to be just like me
But when you tell me that
I don't want you to.
Take the good things
And that's it.
That's why you've never seen me here.
I let you down every time
Even though you have no idea how.
If only you could see my thoughts
When I realize my wrongs.
My eyes become rivers
And my heart falls endlessly.
My embarrassments
Hot like a sun.
And when I keep thinking,
It's all regrets.
I feel
I'll never recover.

I Have A Story To Tell

By Micah, a 14-year-old girl in the shelter at CCYC

I have a story to tell that only I can tell
And my story is....
I met an older man,
He became my boyfriend.
Took my virginity
Then went to jail.
After that I felt lost, hopeless, and used.
To this day I will never let a man
Betray and misuse me.
I did everything I said I'll never do.
Now I'm sitting here writing this like a damn fool.
Make up your mind or be used like a tool.
Life is what you make it,
Never let it be mistaken.
Now the spot is vacant.
It's never too late.
Be on your grind,
Now is the time to shine.
Be open,
And don't no one be unspoken!

CHANGE

Change

Collective poem 7.20.19 from youth in detention at CCYC

Nothing seems to matter.
I'm feeling tired.
In my body I feel
Anxious,
Distorted thoughts.
Ten toes down.
The only constant is change.
There's always a point in time
You have to change.
One day I'll be a free man and I will change.
I'm not going to do the things,
How I used to.
It's harder to do good
Than to be bad.
Shouldn't have to suffer for other people's actions.
More chances.
I want help
To change who I am
And become
The person
I know I am
And
Can be.

Change

Drawing by Lesly Fiarcia

I Need to Change

By Dylan, a 17-year-old in detention at CCYC

I need to change the way I act.
Become a better man.
I need to do something
For my anger.
So it doesn't get the best of me.
It keeps getting me in trouble.
Once I get out of CCYC
I wanna go to counseling
To help me Change
Who I am
And be the person
I know
I am
And Can Be.
And listen to my Dad
Because in the end
He's always right.
I wonder
If I change
Who I am now,
If I will become more successful in my life
And I can be with my family.

I Need to Change

Drawing by Stephanny Calle

I Need to Change

Drawing by Ayam

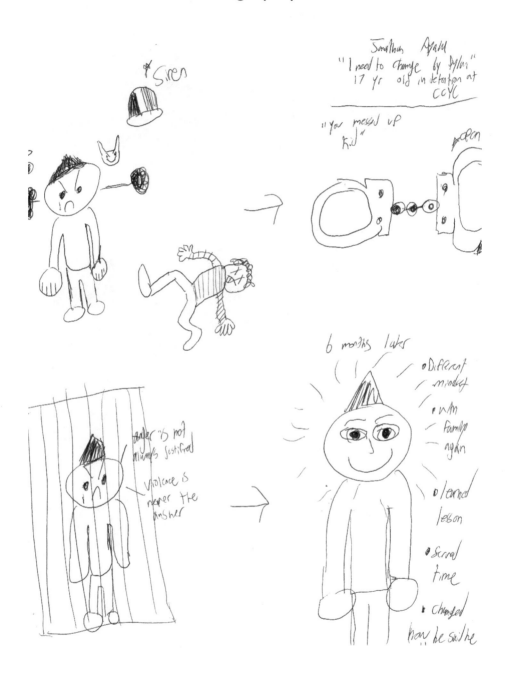

Change

By Mario, a youth in detention at CCYC

Disappointment
Isn't a good feeling
But you can move differently
To make sure that feeling doesn't come back around.
Loss
Isn't something that makes you feel good
But doing things to overcome it
Makes it go away.
Jealousy is always around the corner,
It never goes away.
Inspiration
Will make a weak soul get stronger.
Dreams
Make reality come alive.
Fear
Comes and goes
Just don't let it snatch your soul.
Hope
Barely made it
Change
Always found its way.

Reflection of workshop: "Fear, Jealousy, Inspiration, Change – these words stand out. In my body I feel changes. I realize that there are always opportunities. I wonder what's the next big thing for me."

One Thing

By Mario, a youth in detention at CCYC

One thing that makes me laugh
When people lie.
One thing that challenges me is
Hate.
One thing I am good at is
Helping my people out.
One thing I love about myself is
I never give up.
One thing that makes me happy is
Good vibes.
To succeed in school, I need
To play my role more often.
To succeed in my community, I need
Support.
To succeed in my life, I need
Strength.
If there was one thing
I could change about school it would be
Free dress code.
If there was one thing, I could change about my community it
would be
Poverty.
If there was one thing, I could change about my life it would be
My past.
One thing that I can do now to make a difference is
Change my ways.

One Thing

Drawing by Alanah S.

Title: Into The Unknown

One Thing

By Omar, a youth in detention at CCYC

One thing that makes me laugh
Is the thing I make up with my Imagination.
One thing that challenges me is
My thinking process.
One thing I am good at is
Long board.
One thing I love about myself is
Being a dedicated person to reach my Goals.
One thing that makes me happy is
My nephew.
To succeed in school, I need
To focus on my future career.
To succeed in my community, I need
To change my reputation.
To succeed in my life, I need
To accept criticism
If there was one thing
I could change about school it would be
How segregated it is.
If there was one thing, I could change about my community it
would be
The judgement mentality.
If there was one thing, I could change about my life it would be
The way I choose to have fun
One thing that I can do now to make a difference is
Show empathy.

One Thing

Drawing by Alexandra Monroy

Title: A Film of Life

One Thing

By a collaborative poem by youth in detention at CCYC

One thing that makes me laugh
My mom's corny jokes
Friends,
My girlfriend.
One thing that challenges me is
Life,
Not getting mad,
My thinking process.
One thing I am good at is
Helping my people out,
Braiding hair,
Long boarding.
One thing I love about myself is
I never give up,
I have come this far in life,
My personality.
One thing that makes me happy is
Good vibes,
My nephew,
Being around my friends and family.
My girlfriend.
To succeed in school, I need
A lot of support,
Teachers to understand what we go through
To show up for school.
To succeed in my community, I need
Caring people,
Support,
People to forget about my past,

Change my reputation,
People to stop listening to what other people say about you
Before getting to know you.
To succeed in my life, I need
Strength,
Good and caring people,
If there was one thing, I could change about school it would be
Time,
The kids who go there,
Segregation of groups,
If there was one thing, I could change about my community it
would be
Suffering,
Poverty,
The Judgement mentality,
Prejudice,
More opportunities to connect.
If there was one thing, I could change about my life it would be
My actions in the past.
My past.
One thing that I can do now to make a difference is
Change my ways,
Change my friends that were not the best influence.

One Thing

Drawing by Jeimy M.

Title: Wanting Change

If You Believe

By Nakai a 13-year-old in Detention at CCYC

Continuous-effort.
Not strength
Nor intelligence,
Is the key to unlocking our potential.
If you believe
You can unlock your potential.

We All Matter

There is no one
Who is insignificant
In the purpose of God.
God will always stand by your side,
Because we all matter.

If You Believe

Drawing by Chester County Futures Student

If Only, Only If, Even If

Collaborative Poem written by youth in detention CCYC August 2019

If only I
Didn't get booked,
Didn't leave the house,
Didn't think about myself first.
If only I said
Less,
More,
Said the truth.
If only
He said you will be released.
She said stop.
If only people respected each other
The world would be a better place.
If only people would come together and stop polluting the earth
The world would be a better place.
I can be happy only if
I am true to myself,
Get released and go home.
I can be proud only if I
Accomplish my dreams,
Make my family proud,
Get my legal documents.
I can feel safe only if I
Am with people I trust.
I can change the world only if I change my self.
The world can be better only if we change some laws.
The world can be safer only if we listen to each other.

Cont'd: Collaborative Poem written by youth in detention

EVEN IF
The world is crazy,

I can

Still live life to the fullest.

Still stay strong.

EVEN IF
I make mistakes,

I can

Fix it,

Learn from them.

EVEN IF
Someone tries to bring me down,

I can

Pull myself back up,

Run,

Hold my ground.

EVEN IF
I get hurt or angry,

I can

Walk away,

Push through adversity.

EVEN IF
Life is hard,

I will

Cry,

Chase my dream,

BE RESILIENT.

I Wish, I Want, I Fear, I Hope

By Ameeriah, a girl in the shelter at CCYC

I wish
To be free again
To get all these services out of my life
To see my friends and family soon.
I want
To change
To be successful
To be happy
To go live with my aunt
To go back to real school.
I fear
Being lonely
Being stuck
Being heartbroken.
I hope
My brothers and sisters are okay
That where I'm going is not so bad
I live with my aunt after the RIF.
In my body I feel alone and sad
But I will never show it.
I'm surprised that my mom is starting to care now.
I realized that I cannot go anywhere until I go to RIF.
I feel happy somedays and sad other days.
I'm grateful for CCYC because it is keeping me safe and out of
trouble.

I Wish, I Want, I Fear, I Hope

Drawing by Evelyn Rayon Barrera

LETTERS AND WRITINGS

Letter To My Younger Self

By J, a 15-year-old male in detention

(To my younger self at age 10.)

That is when we started smoking weed and getting in trouble.
I wish I could tell you to stop getting in trouble by doing things that
get you locked up.
You did them because you were bored.
If only there had been more activities like football for young boys
like me in Coatesville.
I started getting in trouble in 5th grade.
I started growing up.
I found others, my peers who were doing bad things.
I wanted to do it to because it was exciting.
Now I know not to do bad things.

Dear Dad

A Youth in detention 9.17.19

I know the last five years have been rough. Trying to work, raise 4 kids, and keep up with the day to day tasks mom always took care of. Life is hopefully getting easier for you. I know it is for the rest of the family, all thanks to you.

I have a lot of respect for you. I always have.

I want you to know, even if I haven't showed it very much recently, I love you.

I want you to know I'm getting help and I'll come home the man you always tell me I can be.

Love,
Your son

Letter to My Son

From Jasmine, a girl in the shelter 8.21.18 at CCYC

Dear Javier,

A.k.a. My son from above.

I love you,

I miss you,

I care about you.

I know I messed up.

I know you're too young to understand.

I'm so sorry for not being around that often

During your months of growing up.

Mommy is going to change.

I will try my hardest

Just for you.

Be brave,

Stay strong.

If I don't get out for your birthday,

Just know I wish you the best wishes

And

The best 1st birthday ever.

Letter To My Son

Drawing by Chester County Futures Student

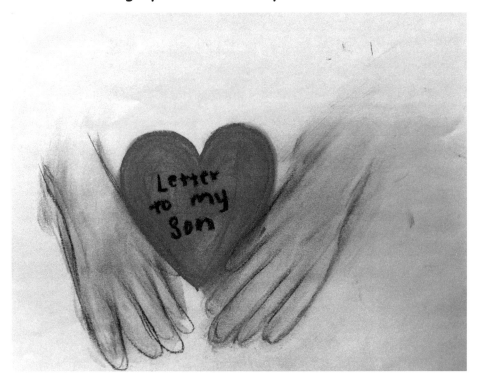

Voices of Restorative Justice Workshop 2 Image Theatre at CCYC 7/13/19

Collaborative Scene

written by residents in workshop 1

What is said out loud
Son
I need to go.
Mom
Please stay, it's not safe.
Son
War isn't safe.
Mom
Don't leave me. Please stay.
Son
I gotta go.

What isn't said out loud but what each of them is thinking
Mom
I'm so afraid something terrible will happen to you.
Son
You think I'm a baby.
Mom
I wish I could lock you in your room.
Son
I hate to make you sad.
Mom
I'm so afraid I can't protect you.

What is said out loud

Mom

I don't like your friends.

They make you feel you need to do things you otherwise wouldn't.

Son

You don't even know them.

All you do is try to control me.

They let me be me.

Mom

And who is it you think you are that I don't see?

I have spent the last 15 years watching you and loving you.

Have they?

Son

I don't want to be what you want.

Mom

Then who do you want to be?

How can I help?

Son

Ok Mom, I'll stay

Later that night the phone rings and the mom gets a call from 911

911 call

Your son is in the ER at the hospital.

His friends have died of an overdose.

Officer John found 6 bags of heroin and 3 needles at the party.

A week later

Son

I'm dealing with a bad court case.

I need your help mom.

Mom

What did you do?

Please tell me the truth

So, I can do the best I can, so you don't get locked up.

What they think but don't say

Son

I'm scared mom

Mom

I love you so much.

I lost your brother.

I don't want to lose you too.

Reflections from participants of the workshop:

"I'm surprised by how wonderful today was and how it brightened my morning and changed my mood to very happy. I didn't think that it was going to be fun and ended up really fun." "I'm surprised how much I wrote." "I realized this was sort of like my story." "In my body I feel like a prisoner tied up who lost control of its body with emotions and sadness taking over." "I wonder who will be thinking about this session throughout the day." "I was surprised of the participation we all had. It was great." "I wonder how many stories we have to tell that start this way." "In my body I feel attached to or close to my character because of the scenarios we have started."

Honesty's Letter To Her Mom

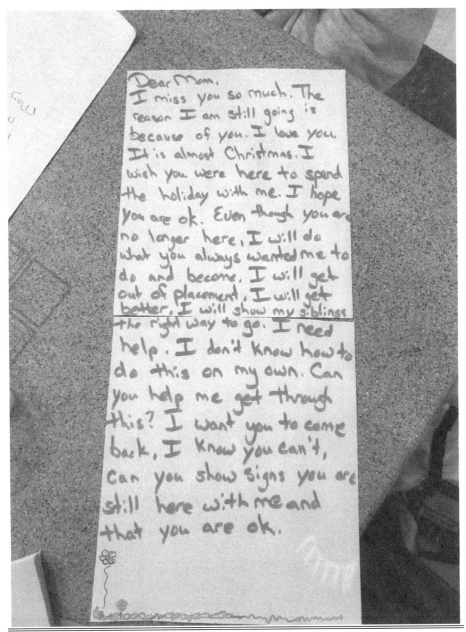

Dear Mom,
I miss you so much. The reason I am still going is because of you. I love you. It is almost Christmas. I wish you were here to spend the holiday with me. I hope you are ok. Even though you are no longer here, I will do what you always wanted me to do and become, I will get out of placement, I will get better, I will show my siblings the right way to go. I need help. I don't know how to do this on my own. Can you help me get through this? I want you to come back, I know you can't, Can you show signs you are still here with me and that you are ok.

Why?

By Steven., a youth in detention at CCYC

Why do fathers disappear?
Why do mothers work so hard?
Why do young men act in front of a crowd of strangers?
Why do girls wear makeup?
Why is love hard to find?
Why is life full of obstacles?
Why do people fear people who bleed?
Why does death make people notice you?
Why do people hate other races?
Why do I need something that brings problems?

Why?

Drawing by Edwin Dominguez

All I Ever Wanted

By Taja, a 16-year-old girl in detention at CCYC

All I ever wanted from my family
Was attention, happiness, love.
I always wanted a bond with my mother
Who I felt abandoned by sometimes,
Even felt like she didn't love me
Or that I was a mistake.
Somedays I even felt like I was the outcast of her family,
I didn't fit in!
All I ever wanted was a conversation or explanation
On why they would make me feel that way!
If I could tell my family how I feel
I would tell them that I feel left out
That I am in a dark hole!
I would tell my mother
That I feel as if me and her should spend more time together.
I would let her know how I feel
I would open up to her more
So that she could understand where I'm coming from.
I would tell her,
Let's take some time, just me and her
So we can get to know each other more.
I would tell her everything.
I would tell her
I'm in a deep dark hole
Sometimes I feel so left out!

All I Ever Wanted

Drawing by Jeihaaira Puigarin

Title: Surrounded Yet Alone

All I Ever Wanted

Drawing by Jaleah

All I Ever Wanted

By Asya a 16-year-old girl in detention at CCYC

All I ever wanted from my family
Was love and happiness.
To be held when I was scared.
To have my family know
That there are better days to come.
I wanted assurance
And not to be mistaken.
I wanted a home that I could go home happy to.
I wanted my mom mostly to be happy
And health.
I wanted my life to be fun and adventures.
I wanted to be free from all negativity.
I want to be home now
And live my life with whoever cares
Or without who doesn't want to be there.

All I Ever Wanted

Drawing by Chester County Futures Student

The Things I'd Like To Understand

A collective poem by Abby, Dhanayah, Hannah, Kayla, Mara, & Wanda
Girls in the shelter at CCYC 6/7/17

The Things I'd Like to Understand:
Why do fathers tease?
Why do fathers have kids and abuse them?
Why do fathers leave their kids and wife?
Why do fathers not claim their own children?
Why are fathers so disrespectful?
Why do mothers care too much?
Why do mothers not understand?
Why do mothers forget we are their babies?
Why do boys act so tough, fight and be so mean?
Why do boys always break girls' hearts?
Why are girls so dramatic?
Why are girls so catty?
Why are girls so fake?
Why do girls believe what others say so easily?
Why is love so hard to find?
Why is love so difficult, so unreliable, so unfair, so unexpected?
Why is love so beautiful?
Why is life so hard?
Why is life so full of pain?
Why is life a mystery and a miracle?
Why does death come so soon?
Why does death happen to innocent people?
Why is death so unexpected?
Why do I learn so slowly?
Why do I act like I'm acting right now?
Why is life so hard to live?
Why is it so hard to maintain a job?
Life is never perfect.
There is always a bad thing in your life.
But never give up,
Get up,
God loves you.

The Things I'd Like To Understand

Picture by Chester County Futures Student

I Wish

By Kayla

Mom,
I wish you knew I have feelings too.
I love attention; I wish you gave me more.
I would open up to you if you listened.
I am emotional.
Regardless, I still love you,
I want a better relationship.
I'm sorry.

I Wish

By Julia

Gail,
I say I don't care what you think.
But, I wish you knew I've been honest with you.
I don't need to be babied.
I'm not having sex with all those guys, like you think I am.
The rumors you've heard, they're not true.
You always think I'm skipping school, and
I wish you knew I do go to school.
I'm a good sister.
I wish you respected that you're not my mom.

I Wish

Drawings by Ariel

I Wish

By Germaly

Dad,

I wish you knew how I feel,

You don't know who I am as a person.

I wish you would do more things with me when you said so.

You give me attitude, so I give you attitude.

I wish I could talk to you about things, but we don't talk like that.

I Wish

Drawing by Ariel

Letter To The Coatesville Community

By Chester County Futures Student

To the Coatesville Community:

Coatesville is my home. Coatesville is where I became the person I am today. Coatesville is a piece of me. Throughout my years in Coatesville, I have been granted the opportunity to become a better person through the experiences I faced day after day. Most days were great for me; however, I can not say the same for others. Through every moment I have seen people fall out of line due to the hardships they faced whether it came from their home or their community. As an 11th grader, I have seen people fall apart due to people not accepting or respecting them. The Coatesville community has shown me that most people do not tend to care about others and would rather be selfish than help another person. One constant I have seen is the discrimination of a group of people. I have witnessed multiple accounts of discrimination against those of different colors and those who identify as members of the LGBTQ community. At the end of the day, we are all people and have the natural right to respect and accept each other for who we are. Instead of arguing with each other and disrespecting each other, we need to come together and grow through the acceptance of everyone in our community. However, I know this is easier said than done. The source of these problems begins with the parents of our community. Just a couple of weeks ago, some of our students had to witness a grown adult brawl in the high school parking lot over a game of basketball. I think all of us can appreciate the amount of spirit these parents have for the sport; however, those acts were unnecessary and unacceptable as they could have been handled in a different manner and environment. Instead of being mature about it, those individuals decided it was perfectly acceptable to take these actions to a school parking lot while students were leaving at the end of the school day. That does not set a good example for the future generations of the Coatesville Community. Ultimately, this is the main failure within our community as all problems can be traced back to the parents. Parents are supposed to teach their children to treat others with respect and to accept everyone for who they are. This has not happened;

as a result, our community is falling apart within and will continue to do so unless something changes with parents' behaviors and influences on their children. To the parents of Coatesville who teach their children to treat others with respect, I'd like to thank you for setting the new generations of Coatesville to become a group of individuals that can make our community stronger than ever. With that being said, Coatesville, it is time for changes and this all starts with the parents. I'd like to thank you for reading this and hopefully, you have a change of heart for the better of all of us in Coatesville.

Letter To Coatesville Education Department

By Anonymous

Dear Coatesville Department of Education and Parents,

We would like to take the time to get your attention with the situations within our community. Consequently, the environment of our community and school haven't placed examples needed for the younger audiences in the Coatesville Community. One topic that I would like to speak about is Mental Health. Mental Health is not something to be ignored about. Kids within our community have certain mental health problems that are pushed away by parents who think it's just a random problem; or just think it's a lie. I happen to be one of those kids. My father grew up in a era where you didn't care about other peoples problems but your own. One day, I was going through a mental breakdown. My father happened to ask me "Why aren't you working as much?" I responded back by saying "I requested off for the days that I have Competition." He scoffed and rolled his eyes. In my mind I didn't really want to talk about anything. He already knew the truth from my mom, but he wanted me to say it. I told him what I said to my mom and also stated that I just needed a mental break. He called me a liar and that there was nothing wrong with me. I stared at him with disbelief, like how could you say something like that to somebody who is having a mental breakdown or problem at that moment. I went to my bedroom and layed in the dark that led me more into my depression that day. Parents, I am begging you to not ignore your childs mental problems, but to instead help them and talk it out with them.

Sincerely,
anonymous

To Parents Of Coatesville

By Devin Hunt

Dear Community and Parents,

Parents have to see that there is more to support in the communities of Coatesville/programs.

Race is a big thing in Coatesville/the world.

Parents need to see that their child/kids need a little more freedom.

Forcing kids to get out of Coatesville because of how things happen, but not saying anything.

All lives matter at the end of the day and adults need to grow up and not kids grow up .

-Devin Hunt

Letter To The Community

By Andrea Lewis

Dear Community,

Be the role model the intercity students need. The hardcore of Coatesville, that do not benefit from the majority that makes up Area School District. Let them be themselves.

-Andrea Lewis

Letter To The Community

By Griffin, a youth in detention at CCYC

Dear Community,
Please learn how to be more accepting
And learn how to treat people that are different than you.
When you look at me
And talk to me
You look and sound
Like I have 5 heads.
Please become more diverse
And find ways to bring people together.
Griffin

About Me: I am transgender and I am waiting for my consultation to begin my transition. I am so excited.

Letter To The Community

By Shanniel, a youth in detention at CCYC

Dear Community,
I need you guys to trust each other.
Care
Love
Each other.
We are all different.
Things are going on in our lives.
We need to stop fighting each other,
Stop stealing from one another,
Stop saying things about other people.
Let's help each other.
I might make mistakes
Here and there
But I can do good things.
Please give me a chance
To show you.
From,
Your boy,
Shanniel

Community

Drawing by Sara Boykin, Teacher, Chester County Futures

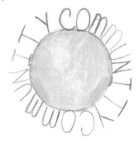

MR. Jarrett Aiken: The Realist

By: M.Y.

You know, a few times in life, you don't see many people take the time to help others or stick by those that care for them, regardless of how much pain they go through. But Mr. Jarrett Aiken was one of those people I thought of as not just a man who cared, but one of the realest men I've ever met in my life. I still remember when my brother, Z.Y., traveled to Texas and went to an event with Ebony A. One of the greatest moments of my life was when I overheard my mother, S.Y., talk about how Mr. Jarret practically made brother become a gentleman. Opening the door for Ebony the whole time he was down there and escorting her. That shaped me into the gentleman I am now and it taught me a valuable lesson, "Be a gentleman on every date you go on, even if that person ain't grateful for it. From that point on, I took that lesson with me on every date I've ever been on. But the best thing about Mr. Jarrett was not just his teaching, but his listening. Whenever I had problems at home, he would find out and he would talk with me, even when I wanted to isolate myself from everyone because I was so mad. He was the only person I could talk to that would be 1000% real with me no matter how bad the situation was or sounded. I remember all those times I talked with him and sometimes my mother would be in the same room and he'd talk to both of us. Even though she can be a huge headache and talk more than an auctioneer, she was great friends with him and she loved him and the whole family. But, the one conversation I'll never forget was when he said, "I can't get with a lie." It was hard for me to talk to almost anyone and everyone about my problems because I felt like nobody would take my side and/or think of me as a villain. When really I was just a young bull who's seen this world take a look at one African American and instantly take the opposite side without giving a rat's behind about what they have to say, even if they telling the truth. I felt like when I was younger, he was the only person I could truly express myself towards without the fear of being stripped of anything or coming across as the second coming of the late great legend and one of my role models, DMX, who would lash out at people or cuss them out. I share this with you all because he guided me through the bad parts in my life, all those times where I was too mad to even talk with my family and instead lie to them and ghost them. He showed me how to open myself more and express my truth and how I really feel. Along with DMX, which is why I looked up to and admired him. Even though I'm still working through those challenges, I don't wanna lie to anybody, regardless of what they might think of me, say about me, or even do to me. Even if they did me like they did the five innocent black children who were incarcerated for something they didn't even do in 1989. like Trip Lee and Lecrae, "I'm Good" because the Lord is my coach and my passion for him shines brighter than a trillion stars in the sky. So for all the friends, family, and everyone that loved Mr. Jarrett, I want y'all to do me a favor. Remember him, celebrate him, be inspired by him, because he's watching over all of us and like Phil Collins, he'll be in your hearts and in mine forever more. Don't run away from the bad parts of your life because they make you who and what you're supposed to become. Don't be afraid to express how you really feel because the Lord is real, he's king, he rules, he's unstoppable, and protective over all who believe in him and worship him for all eternity. More importantly, remember that somehow, someway, someday, the truth always sees the light of day. Mr. Jarrett, you were and always will be the epitome of a real one and I was very, very, very blessed to have you in my life as a friend and a mentor. I really don't care if I go through hell the last few months of my college career, I'll make you proud and get my degree. Goodbye.

RIP JARRETT AIKEN

From Yours Truly,
"Matty Ice"

P.S- Tell Kobe Bryant, Robin Williams, and DMX that I'm a big fan of theirs.

"Celebrate for the ones we lost here, Celebrate for the ones we got here."

ARTIST STATEMENT

Chester County Futures, Teacher and Students

* Sara Boykin is a Chester County Futures teacher on a mission to encourage all bodies to feel empowered no matter where they are on their journey through yoga and holistic nutritional wellness. She currently holds a BA in Psychology, yoga teacher certification, and training in trauma-informed approaches. Sara is currently working on her yoga therapy certification and studying holistic health. In her down time, she enjoys hiking, especially when there are waterfalls, traveling, and crafting.

* Evelyn Rayon-Barrera – I'm currently a junior and had a rough journey. When I was $1\frac{1}{2}$ years young I lost my father to an accident. My mom a hard worker, had to be a single mom. Anything I do will be for her, I love her and she's my motivation. I love you mom.

* Edwin Dominguez – My name is Edwin Dominquez. I am a junior at Oxford Area High School with high interest in soccer and math. I plan on pursuing my education as an engineer in the future. I've grown to be responsible and respectful. I am more than thankful for my father for teaching me valuable aspects of life.

* Jahaaira Pulgorin – I'm 17 years old, a Jr. in high school and the last child from 3. My family is from Ecuador we visit every 2-3 years. My parents didn't get the chance to go to college because of financial problems and rights after they graduated high school in Ecuador. They came over here to start a family and give us what they never had growing up. Till this day my parents make sure we have everything we need, make sure we reach our limits, push us to be the best we can, and follow our dreams. For all they have done in these 17 years I want to

thank them because everything I ever did and overcame was because of them.

* Jeimy Montero-Acosta – I'm an 18-year-old girl from Kennett Square. I enjoy baking and drawing or just being creative.
* Stephanny Calle - ¡Cree en ti!
* Emanuel Mendiola Ortiz – I am from Mexico. I am a senior graduating from Kennett High School. I will be going to Penn State University (University Park) as a first-generation student, majoring in Information Sciences and Technology. My favorite things to do is go outside, spend time with family and watch movies.
* Dario Duran – I am a 17-year-old from Kennett Square, PA. Never had depression but have always been surrounded by people who do. So, I tried to portray what I've seen in a drawing.
* D – Thanks to my mom's boyfriend, I would not have the knowledge I have today, or I wouldn't be the man I am. I am loving, caring, and loyal. I am fearless and patient.
* J- Realize everyone ain't loyal.
* C.C – I am a 17-year-old male from Harrisburg, PA. I dedicate this to my daughter, and I am thankful for my very supportive family.
* L.N – Thanks to my parents I wouldn't be the person I am today.
* Samantha Martinez – I am a Kennett Highschool junior who wishes to pursue a career in Early Childhood to help be a role model for my younger students.
* Alexandra Monroy – Hi, I'm Alexandra but I go by Ali. I'm a 16-year-old Mexican girl living in Kennett Square. Art to me is a gate to freedom. It's a way to express myself and present myself.

* Karen Juarez-Hernandez – I'm 17 years old and have lived in Kennett Square all my life. I'm very passionate about helping others.
* Emma Zahira Urrutia Vela – Hi there! I'm Emma, I am currently 17 years old. I am a junior in high school. After high school I am planning on attending college and have a successful future to not only benefit me but successful enough to help and care for my parents.
* April Aguilera – My name is April Aguilera. I am 17 years old. I plan on becoming an ultrasound tech. I enjoy listening to music and reading in my free time. I hope to go to West Chester University.
* Estrella Martinez – I'm a junior at Kennett High School. In the future I want a profession in the law field. Surrounding myself around people who encourage and believe in me is something that has helped me throughout the years.
* Jocelyn Espinoza – I'm an eleventh-grade student and in the future, I hope to major in criminology. All throughout high school I have strived to do my best to accomplish my goals in life. With the support of my mom, I have been able to accomplish many things.
* Yesenia Ramirez – I am from Borrosow, Kentucky. I am the upcoming first graduate in my family from three other generations. One wisdom, the smallest feature within one, may have the most meaningful meaning behind. We all have our stories.
* Mariana Sanchez-Lara and I am a junior in high school. Attending a four-year university for business or architecture is part of my future aspirations.
* Bryannah Moore - My name is Bryannah Moore, I'm from Coatesville, P.A. I would like to thank Josh, Jordan, and Mr.

Jack Crans for always providing a fun and safe space for kids in my community.

★ Yanessa Santana – I am a 17-year-old girl, who has to survive in a world of judgement. I don't change who I am for nobody because I love myself and I know when to keep it professional.

★ Ivy Cooper – I'm a junior from CASH and I also do the marketing and finances. I'm a dancer on CMS Elite All Stars Cheer and Dance. In 10 years, I see myself with a dance studio in Georgia.

★ Jaleah – Hello! My name is Jaleah, and I am from Coatesville, PA! I enjoy reading, spending time with my family, and collecting sneakers!

★ Kiara Carrillo – I'm a junior in high school and I hope that in the future I'm helping others and being a voice for people that don't feel heard. I'm not sure how but I know I will.

★ M. Torres- I am a senior getting ready for college next year, with the goal of earning a business degree. I am thankful for my older brother for always being there for me every step of the day.

★ Kaily Ortega – I'm a senior in high school. Love making people laugh. Love having a good time. I am thankful for my mom. She has always wanted what's best for me.

★ Lesly Garcia – I am a senior in high school and am planning to go to college for Psychology. I am a first-generation student in my family. Someone who inspires me is my psychology teacher Ms. Basia, who pushes me to follow my dreams and be better.

★ Abby Rodriguez – I am a senior at Oxford Area High School. I enjoy doing activities like shot put, cheer, band, and singing. I would describe myself as outgoing, hardworking, and motivated. I am inspired by and thankful for my mom.

* Claudia Vara – Shoutout to Stephanny Calle for keeping me on track these four years.
* Michaella Remy- I am Michaella Remy. I am currently attending Coatesville Area Senior High School. I plan on going to college to pursue my major on Cybersecurity. I am musically talented, enjoy reading, and playing instruments.
* Kevin Zavalazavak – I am a high school student at Kennett High School that would like to pursue a career in computer science or software engineering. I love to play sports, play guitar, and lift. I play football, run track, and I wrestle.
* Alazia Hudnell – I am a senior at Coatesville Area Senior High School. I plan on majoring in Psychology in college, in order to help the people around me. Shoutout to my mom for always motivating me and never letting me give up.
* Andrea Lewis – Growing up Black in a world that doesn't accept you. "Don't hang with them," words from someone that is trying to convey that if you befriend them, you will become them, what they don't care about is why they are the way they are. I get to be written off as the golden child because I check off "all the acceptable boxes."
* Rubyt Luna-Hernandez – Hello. I'm a senior at the Kennett High School. Currently received Veterinary assist and training. Just a regular student who separates dog fights as a job.

West Chester University Students

★ My name is Christine Schmitt, I am a junior at West Chester University. I am Criminal Justice major with a minor in Law,

Politics and Society. I am so grateful to be a part of the Honors college that allowed me to work as the team leader on this project. This has only fueled my passion to end the injustices in the Criminal legal system. I hope reading *Justice Restored 3.0* breaks the stereotypes many of us have on juveniles that are involved and work towards becoming a more empathetic, trauma informed society.

★ Dayla Fuselli - I'm a Finance and Economics Major at West Chester University. I am involved in the Honors program, which

allowed me to have the exclusive opportunity of reading and sorting through poems and writings done by children at the Chester County Youth Center. While working on the *Justice Restored 3.0* project, I felt that I was impacted in a way I had not expected. These children have beautiful minds and were able to create touching works of art. I am thankful to be involved with this project, and I look forward to my next opportunity to help our youth in the area.

* Briaira - I'm a third year Finance and Econ major at WCU. My favorite quote is "Happiness is not by chance, but by choice." I

really enjoyed working on *Justice Restored 3.0*. It was a great experience, and I was happy to see compassionate people working with incarcerated youth.

* Liz Stewart - I'm a junior in college. I loved working alongside *Justice Restored 3.0* and am eager to read the new published book of poems/short stories

ACKNOWLEDGEMENTS

AHHAH would like to thank Chester County Youth Center (CCYC) in West Chester, PA for allowing us to conduct Expressive Arts workshops for the Justice Restored book series. Thank you to all the young residents at the center for sharing their stories, their poems, their lives with us and the reader.

Thank you to the team of students lead by Christine Schmitt, a student in Dr. Matt Saboe's West Chester University's Honors Economics class fall of 2021. Dr. Saboe's class studies the impact of poverty, race, and mass incarceration on our society. A team of 6 students read over 500 pieces written by CCYC youth between 2017 and 2021 and selected 50 of these pieces for inclusion in the third edition of *Justice Restored*.

AHHAH would like to thank Chester County Futures (CCF) in Coatesville, Kennett, and Oxford, PA who, in collaboration with AHHAH's Director of Expressive Arts, Zandra Matthews, created the illustrations for the poems written by CCYC youth. The CCF students were so moved by the letters and poems they read, they asked to write letters to the community and the school board to express their feelings. Their writings are also included in this book.

AHHAH also wishes to thank Lori Cushman and the Justamere Foundation for their support and donations to the youth workshops that made this publication possible.

Lastly, AHHAH thanks Paul Salvo, Founder of Bushwick Writer Publishing, who worked closely with Zandra Matthews, AHHAH's Director of Expressive Arts, on arranging and editing the contents of *Justice Restored 3.0*.

Made in the USA
Columbia, SC
25 September 2024

42798317R00070